101 Facts

Roller Coasters

Explore the History, Science, and Most Famous Roller Coasters Around the World

Nick Weisenberger

First Edition – Paperback Version

Copyright ©2024 by Nick Weisenberger

ISBN: 9798345899434

Imprint: Independently published

All rights reserved. No part of this book may be reproduced or transmitted in any form or by any means, electronic or mechanical, including photocopying, recording, or by any information storage and retrieval system, without permission in writing by the author. The only exception is by a reviewer, who may quote short excerpts in a review.

Although the author has attempted to exhaustively research all sources to ensure the accuracy and completeness of information on the subject matter, the author assumes no responsibility for errors, inaccuracies, omissions, or any other inconsistencies herein. No affiliation with, or endorsed by anyone associated, or in any way connected with any amusement park, company, or product listed herein. Any perceived slight of any individual or organization is purely unintentional. We recognize that some words, model names and designations, for example, mentioned herein are the property of the trademark owner. We use them for identification purposes only. This is not an official publication.

Readers should also be aware that internet websites listed in this work may have changed or disappeared between when this work was written and when it is read.

This book belongs to:

Table of Contents

Welcome to the Wonderful World of Roller Coasters!..............................5

Roller Coaster Terminology..8
Roller Coaster History..21
How Roller Coasters Work..30
Record Holders and Famous Roller Coasters........................47
Roller Coaster Trivia..61
Roller Coaster Trivia Answers..69

Trivia Score 72

Enjoy the Ride..81

About the Author...84

Books by Nick Weisenberger 85

Resources 86

Photography Credits 87

Welcome to the Wonderful World of Roller Coasters!

Have you ever felt the rush of speeding down a track, the wind in your face, with your heart pounding in excitement? That's what riding a roller coaster is all about! Roller coasters are more than just thrilling rides – they're amazing creations of engineering, science, and imagination that give people the feeling of flying, falling, and twisting in all directions. Roller coasters have been around for over 200 years, from simple ice slides evolving into the high-speed thrill rides we know today.

In this book, we're going to explore 101 incredible facts about roller coasters that will make you see these rides in a whole new way. Here's what you'll find in this book:

- **History and Famous Coasters**: Discover where roller coasters first started, learn about famous ones like Kingda Ka, and see how coasters have changed over time.
- **The Science of Thrills**: Find out how roller coasters work, what makes them safe, and why you feel weightless at the top of a bunny hill.
- **Record Holders**: Meet some of the wildest record-breaking coasters around the world, including the tallest, fastest, and longest ones!

Each fact has been meticulously researched. However, it should be noted that the statistics and numbers mentioned in this book are based on records as of November 2024. New roller coasters that push the limits of what is possible are built every year and the current record holders are subject to change.

By the end of this book, you'll be a mini-expert in roller coasters, knowing cool facts about famous rides, how they work, and the science behind why they're so thrilling. You'll even be able to impress your friends with your knowledge next time you go to an amusement park!

So, buckle up, hold on tight, and get ready for a wild ride into the awesome world of roller coasters!

Screamin' Eagle at Six Flags St. Louis

Roller Coaster Terminology

1. What is a roller coaster? Anything at an amusement park that makes you scream your head off, right? Not quite. A **roller coaster** is defined as a passenger carrying vehicle that rolls along one or more rails primarily due to gravity.

2. Roller coasters are classified as one of three types: **wooden, steel, and hybrid**. You'll soon see that roller coaster fans love to give everything a name.

3. **Steel** roller coasters are defined as a roller coaster with a track consisting of steel rails. The rails can be any shape so long as they are made completely of steel. The most common type of steel coaster track uses round tubes or pipes.

4. **Wooden** roller coasters are made with tracks built

from layers of strong, laminated wood, called "the stack". This stack is what makes it a wooden coaster, not the type of support underneath. Most wooden coasters have thin strips of steel on top of the stack for the wheels to smoothly run on. *The Voyage* at Holiday World in Santa Claus, Indiana, is a wooden track coaster held up by a steel lattice structure.

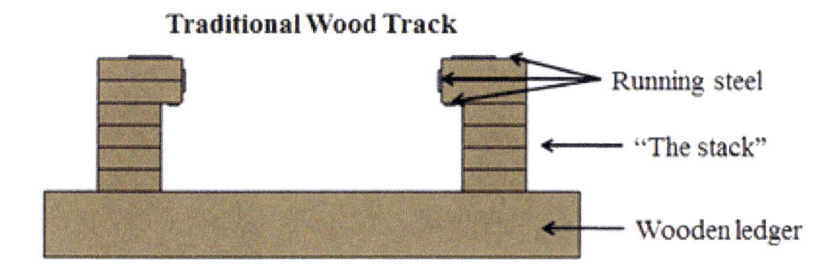

Traditional Wood Track

Running steel
"The stack"
Wooden ledger

5. A relatively new class of roller coaster is the **hybrid**, where the line between steel and wood coasters has become blurred. Wooden coasters have more steel components than ever before. Some traditionally defined wooden coasters have had steel track installed in the high stress areas of the ride transforming them into true hybrid coasters. Some roller coasters, like Steel Vengeance at Cedar Point, are considered hybrids because they have steel tracks but are supported by a wooden structure.

6. An uninterrupted closed loop path or track is called a **full-circuit** roller coaster. Like a racetrack.

7. A roller coaster where the track is not a complete circuit is called a **shuttle coaster**. Flash: Vertical Velocity at Six Flags Great America in Gurnee, Illinois is a great example of a shuttle coaster.

8. The average length of a roller coaster, distance wise, is around 3,000 feet (or 915 meters).

9. A **hyper coaster** is any roller coaster that is between 200 feet (61 meters) and 299 feet tall, like Mamba at Worlds of Fun.

10. Any roller coaster between 300 (91 meters) and 399 feet tall is called a **giga coaster.** Orion at Kings

Island is often debated among fans if it is truly a giga coaster as it is only 287 feet tall but has a 300-foot drop.

11. **Strata coasters** are coasters over 400 feet tall (122 meters), such as Kingda Ka at Six Flags Great Adventure and Top Thrill 2 at Cedar Point.

12. A coaster's **layout** refers to the specific design of the track and elements. Roller coasters with the same layout are referred to as **clones**.

13. An **element** is a segment of coaster track that curves in a recognizable shape. Elements are often given names such as corkscrew, loop, cobra roll, dive loop, etc.

14. An inversion element like a loop except the entrance and exit points have been stretched apart is called a **corkscrew**.

15. A **cobra roll** is a double inversion element. A

half-loop followed by half a corkscrew, then another half corkscrew into another half-loop. The trains are inverted twice and exit the element in the opposite direction from which they entered.

A corkscrew element (left) and a cobra roll (right)

16. **Headchopper** moments are points where riders feel as though they're narrowly missing an overhead object, like they might get their head chopped off.

17. A **racing coaster** has two separate tracks that

are usually parallel for most of the course. Trains are released simultaneously so they race from start to finish.

18. A **dueling coaster** is similar to a racing coaster where there are two separate tracks but they are mostly not parallel. They usually contain several head-on, near miss collision sensations. Some roller coasters, like Lightning Racer at HersheyPark, both race and duel.

The offset lift hills of Lightning Racer at HersheyPark

19. A line you stand in for an attraction, food, or entry/exit is called the **queue** (not queue line as that would be redundant).

20. Skip the line passes, often called **fast passes**, let you wait less for rides at theme parks. Normally, people line up to wait their turn, sometimes for a long time, especially on popular rides. But with a fast pass, you get to use a special, shorter line so you can get on the ride quicker! This pass helps you fit in more fun rides without spending as much time waiting around. Some amusement parks offer free fast passes, but most now require an additional fee on top of the cost of the ticket to enter the park.

21. The term **coaster enthusiast** is often used to describe dedicated fans who travel long distances to experience new rides. Non-roller coaster enthusiasts are often referred to as "GP" or "General Public."

22. In 2007, schoolteacher and roller coaster

superfan Richard Rodriguez rode the Pepsi Max Big One and Big Dipper roller coasters at Pleasure Beach, Blackpool, United Kingdom for 405 hours and 40 minutes from July 27th to August 13th. Richard ate, drank, and slept on the coaster and donated funds raised through the record attempt to diabetes research.

23. According to Guinness World Records, the greatest number of different roller coasters ridden in one 24-hour period is 74. This was achieved by a team of four individuals - Philip A Guarno, Adam Spivak, John R Kirkwood, and Aaron Monroe Rye - on August 9, 2001, where they rode coasters across 10 amusement parks in four US states, utilizing helicopters for travel between locations.

24. Roller coasters come in many different seating arrangements and configurations. **Stand-up coasters** allow riders to stand, supported by a bicycle-style seat and over-the-shoulder restraints.

Pipeline: The Surf Coaster at SeaWorld Orlando is the latest standup coaster in the United States and simulates the feeling of standing on a surfboard.

The lone inversion on Pipeline: The Surf Coaster

25. **Floorless coasters** allow riders' feet to dangle *above the track*. The first floorless coaster was Medusa at Six Flags Great Adventure, and opened in 1999 (rethemed as Bizarro from 2009 – 2021).

26. **Suspended roller coasters** have cars hanging below track. Some suspended coasters have cars that can swing from side to side. **The Bat** at Kings Island was the world's first suspended coaster but closed due to technical issues. The original Bat operated from 1981 to 1983. A new suspended coaster opened at Kings Island in 1993, originally called Top Gun but renamed Bat in 2014, operates to this day.

27. Suspended roller coasters with non-swinging cars are also called **inverted coasters**. Inverted coaster seating allows rider's feet to hang freely, but the cars are below the track, not above them, so they are not floorless.

Freedom Flyer suspended coaster at Fun Spot America

28. A **spinning coaster** has cars that spin around on a vertical axis during the ride, adding an unpredictable element.

Tidal Twist spinning coaster at the Columbus Zoo

29. **Bobsled** coaster cars travel freely down a U-shaped track (no rails) like a bobsled, except on wheels - no ice needed!

30. A **flying roller coaster** is a type of ride where you can experience what it feels like to soar through the air, almost like you're a superhero or a bird! Unlike other roller coasters where you sit upright, a

flying coaster has special seats that tilt you forward, so you're facing the ground with your body parallel to the track. When the ride starts, it lifts you into this "flying" position, making you feel like you're gliding over hills, diving through loops, and swooping around curves. Flying coasters are primarily made by B&M or Vekoma.

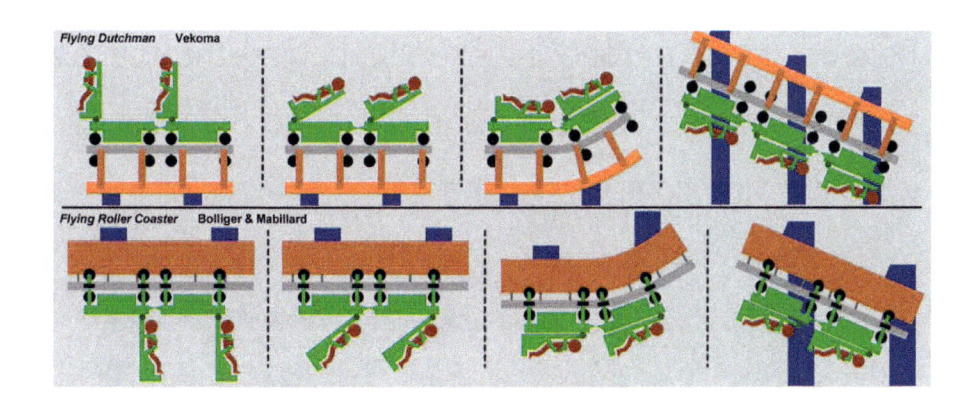

31. **ERT** stands for **Exclusive Ride Time**. It's a special time when only a small group of people, like a fan club or event participants, get to ride a roller coaster or other rides without waiting in long lines. ERT usually happens before the park opens or after it closes to regular visitors, which means way less

waiting and more time to ride your favorite coasters over and over.

32. **The American Coaster Enthusiasts (ACE)** is a non-profit organization that promotes the appreciation, enjoyment, and preservation of roller coasters. ACE was founded in 1978 and has over 7,000 members worldwide. ACE members receive benefits such as special events, behind-the-scenes tours, exclusive discounts, and invites to new coaster openings and commercial shoots.

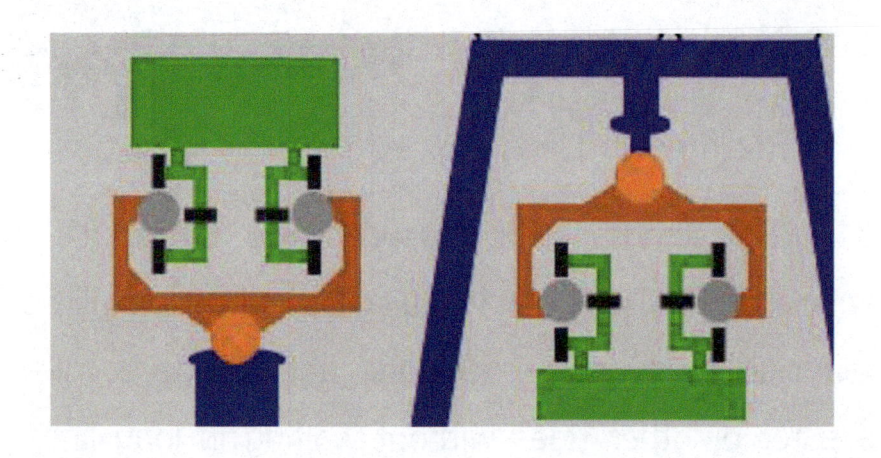

A coaster car above the track (left) and below the track (right)

Roller Coaster History

33. Roller coasters originated in Russia in the 1600s as ice slides built on wooden frames and called **Russian Mountains**.

34. The first roller coaster on wheels was built in the Gardens of Oreinabum in St. Petersburg, Russia in 1784.

35. The Aerial Walk (*Promenades Aeriennes*) was the first full-circuit roller coaster, meaning the track was an uninterrupted closed path.

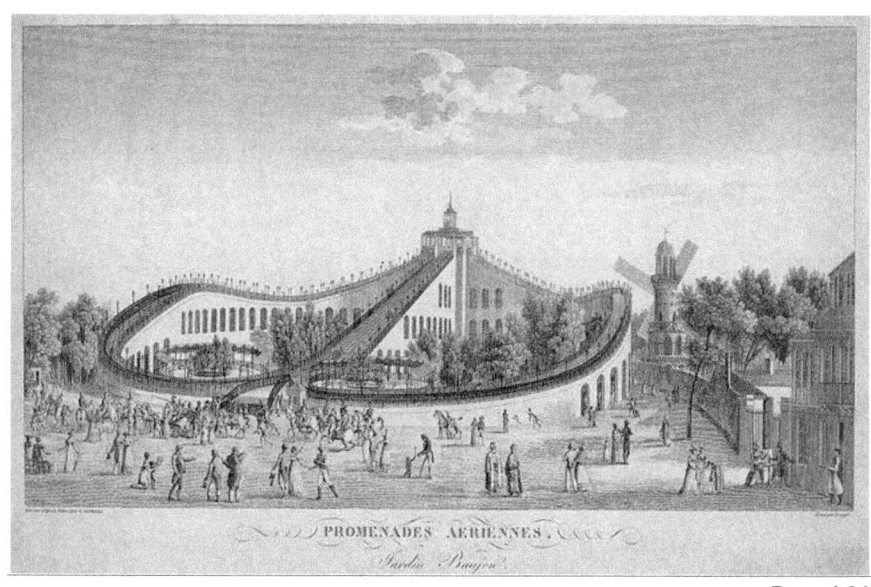

36. The Centrifugal Railway in Frascati Garden, Paris in 1846 was the first looping roller coaster (though it was not a full circuit).

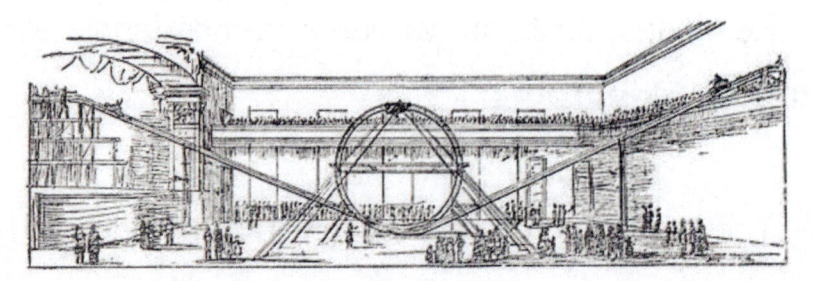

37. The Mauch Chunk Railway was a coal-hauling railroad that became the prototype for roller coasters in the United States. Built in 1873 in Pennsylvania, it was the second most visited attraction in America behind Niagara Falls.

38. Thompson's Switchback Railway opened in 1884 at Coney Island in Brooklyn, New York and was the

first ground-up roller coaster built in America.

39. The first use of lap bar restraints was in 1907 on the Drop-the-Dips at Coney Island in Brooklyn, New York.

40. The 1920s are considered the Golden Age of roller coasters, with over 1,500 built.

41. In 1925, the Revere Beach Cyclone became the first roller coaster to break the one-hundred-foot-tall barrier.

42. The Depression and World War II caused many parks and coasters to close during the 1930s and 1940s.

43. The Matterhorn Bobsleds opened at Disneyland in Anaheim, California in 1959 and was the first tubular steel rail coaster. It also used a modern control system to keep the cars from running into one another.

44. Wooden double roller coaster, *The Racer* at Kings Island, sparked a revival of roller coasters in 1972.

45. The first launch coaster, King Kobra, opened at Kings Dominion in Doswell, Virginia in 1977. The coaster used a weight drop to launch the trains to full speed rather than the traditional chain lift hill.

46. The first coaster to use stand-up trains opened in Japan in 1982. Today, there are currently only eight operating standup coasters in the world.

47. In 1989, Magnum Xl-200 at Cedar Point in Sandusky, Ohio became the first full-circuit roller coaster to break the 200-foot barrier.

48. Batman: The Ride at Six Flags Great America introduced the first inverted roller coaster in 1992.

49. Opened in 1996, Flight of Fear at Kings Island was the first roller coaster to use electromagnets, called linear induction motors, to launch the trains.

50. A roller coaster reaching speeds of 100 mph? It was unthinkable. That is, until Superman: The Escape opened in 1997 at Six Flags Magic Mountain in Valencia, California. With the use of linear synchronous motors (LSMs) the car is accelerated from zero to 100 mph in seven heart-pounding seconds. LSMs use the basic magnetism theories of attraction and repulsion.

51. Hop Hari in San Paolo, Brazil opened in 1999 and was South America's first wooden roller coaster.

52. Also in 1999, Superman: Ride of Steel at Six Flags Darien Lake near Buffalo, New York was the first roller coaster to use magnetic braking.

53. In 2000, Millennium Force at Cedar Point in Sandusky, Ohio became the first full-circuit roller coaster to stand over 300 feet tall. It also was the first modern coaster to utilize a cable lift rather than a chain.

The 310-foot-tall lift hill of Millennium Force

54. Son of Beast was a wooden roller coaster at Kings Island in Mason, Ohio that was the tallest, fastest, and first wooden hyper coaster in the world

when it opened in 2000. It was also the first wooden coaster in the modern era to feature a vertical loop. Sadly, issues with the massive ride's design and construction caused the ride to be closed in 2009 and dismantled in 2012.

55. In 2003, just a few short years after the record setting Millennium Force debuted, Cedar Point launched Top Thrill Dragster, the first full-circuit coaster to stand over 400 feet tall. Top Thrill Dragster used a hydraulic motor connected to a cable to launch you from zero to 120 miles per hour in under four seconds! Top Thrill Dragster closed in 2021.

56. Falcon's Flight is an unimaginable roller coaster set to open in 2025 at the new Six Flags Qiddiya City in Saudi Arabia. It will not only set but absolutely smash the world records for tallest, fastest, and longest roller coaster. The highest point above the ground will be 540 feet (165 meters) with a total

difference of 640 feet (195 meters) between the lowest and highest points. The top speed will be a blistering 155.3 miles per hour (250 km/h). The track length will be 13,123 feet (4,000 meters). The ride is so big they had to make up a new classification to describe it: **the Exa Coaster!**

57. At the time of this writing, there are **5,871** operating roller coasters throughout the world, with more under construction. Think of it this way: if you could ride one new roller coaster every day, it would take you over 16 years to ride them all! That's almost as long as it takes to go from kindergarten to graduating high school.

How Roller Coasters Work

58. A **force** is a push or pull that can make an object start moving, stop, change direction, or change shape. Forces are measured in newtons (N). Forces work by causing objects with mass to accelerate (change speed or direction) according to Newton's laws of motion. For example, when you push a toy car, the force of your hand makes it move. There are many types of forces, like gravity (which pulls things down toward Earth), friction (which slows things down), and magnetic force (which pulls or pushes magnets and certain metals).

59. **G-force**, or gravitational force, refers to the feeling of "weight" or "pressure" due to acceleration, often compared to Earth's gravity. One G is the force we feel due to Earth's gravity when standing still (1 G = 9.8 meters/second^2). G-force measures the intensity of force felt as acceleration changes. For instance, on a roller coaster, you feel G-forces as it

speeds up, slows down, or changes direction. A 2 G experience would make you feel twice as heavy as you do standing still.

59. **Friction** is a force that resists relative motion (sliding or rolling) of an object. Friction is a force that happens when two surfaces rub against each other, and it works to slow things down or make it harder for them to move. Even though surfaces may look smooth, if you look very closely, you'd see they actually have tiny bumps and rough spots. When two surfaces slide against each other, these little bumps catch on each other, creating friction.

60. Roller coasters are all about managing the relationship between potential and kinetic energy. **Potential energy** is *stored* and based on position, while **kinetic energy** is the *energy of motion*. Objects can shift between these types of energy, like a roller coaster at the top of a hill (high potential energy) zooming down the hill (converting to kinetic

energy). In other words, potential energy is like "waiting energy," and kinetic energy is "moving energy.

61. A **lift hill** is a mechanism used to transport a roller coaster car or train up a hill to an elevated point. As the train is pulled to the top, it is gaining potential energy, or stored energy. Once released, the acceleration due to gravity makes the vehicles coast back to the station as the potential energy is turned into kinetic energy. Roller coaster cars are pulled up a lift hill by either a chain or a cable. The lift hill is usually the first and tallest hill on a roller coaster (but not always).

62. A **launch coaster** is a type of roller coaster that uses a powerful launch system to quickly accelerate riders to high speeds, often right out of the station or from a standstill on the track. Instead of the traditional chain lift hill that slowly pulls the train up, a launch coaster propels the train forward at rapid speeds in seconds, creating an adrenaline-packed start to the ride.

63. The most common type of launch coasters use electromagnetics, either LIMs or LSMs, to launch roller coasters super-fast! Here's how they work:

LIM (Linear Induction Motor): Imagine a powerful magnetic "push." LIMs use magnets to create a strong magnetic force that moves the roller coaster car forward. The magnets in the track attract and repel the magnets on the car, giving it a big push, sort of like a slingshot! This makes the coaster speed up fast.

LSM (Linear Synchronous Motor): LSMs are also magnetic but are even more precise and powerful.

With LSM, the magnets are set up to push and pull the coaster car in a super smooth, controlled way. It's like getting a boost that's both strong and steady, so the car can reach high speeds quickly but smoothly.

64. Roller coaster cars often run on wheels positioned in three places: the **road wheels** are positioned above the track and carry the majority of the weight. **Upstop wheels** are located below the track and help keep it secured to the track. Side friction wheels or **guide wheels** are located on either side of the rails to help steer the cars.

65. Roller coaster wheels are typically made from polyurethane or a blend of nylon and polyurethane. The wheels are usually made up of an aluminum hub with a polyurethane tire bonded to the outside. The choice of material for roller coaster wheels depends on the desired ride performance. For example, nylon is a hard plastic that offers low rolling resistance (less friction) and durability, but it can be more demanding on the track and may cause vibrations. Polyurethane is a softer plastic that provides a smoother ride with less vibration than nylon, but it also results in a slower ride (more friction). Some amusement parks use a combination of both nylon and polyurethane wheels.

66. An **anti-rollback** (or ARB) on a roller coaster is a safety feature that prevents the coaster cars from rolling backwards down the lift hill, especially in case of a power failure or chain malfunction. The coaster train has a special piece of metal called an "anti-rollback dog" that drops down into the grooves

of the teeth on the track as the train ascends. The clicking noise you often hear while going up the lift hill is usually the sound of the anti-rollback dogs engaging with the teeth in the track.

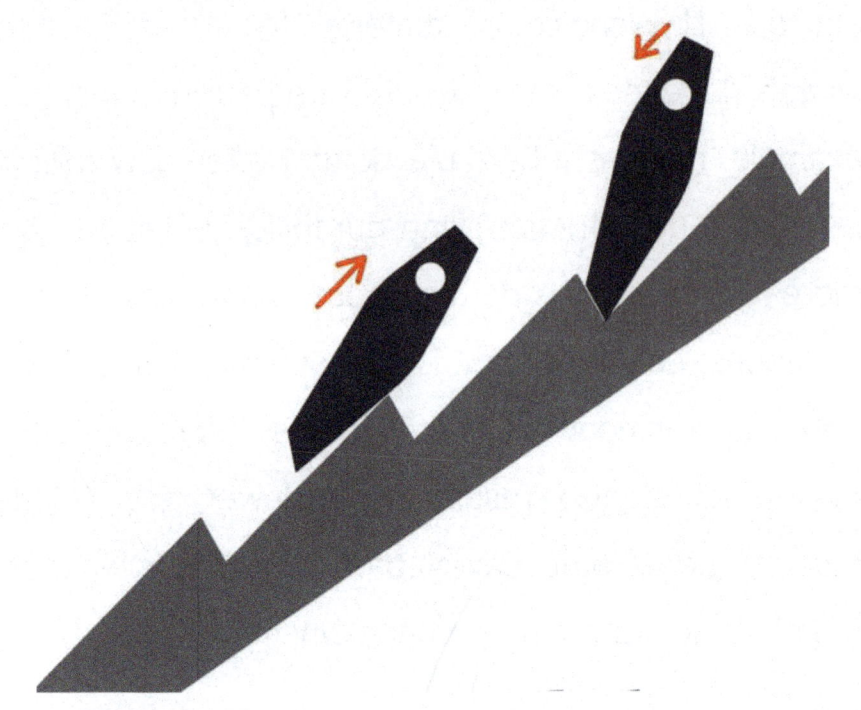

67. Roller coasters are able to safely operate multiple trains on the same track due to block zones. A **block** is a section of a roller coaster's track with a controllable start and stop point. Only one train may occupy a block at a time. Roller coaster cars typically do not have any brakes or way to stop on them; the

brakes are located on the tracks but only in certain areas.

68. **Friction Brakes** and **Magnetic Brakes** are both used to slow down roller coasters, but they operate differently.

Friction brakes work by creating direct contact between two surfaces, usually through brake pads that press against a moving part of the vehicle, like a metal rail or wheel. The friction created as the surfaces rub together slows down the ride. However, they create a lot of heat, which can cause wear on the parts over time, requiring regular maintenance.

Magnetic brakes use the repelling force of magnets to create a smooth, friction-free braking effect. When magnets on the ride's track interact with magnets or metal fins on the coaster, they create resistance that slows down the train without any contact. However, since the magnetic braking force is proportional to the speed of the vehicle, magnetic brakes cannot bring the car to a complete stop.

In many modern roller coasters, both systems are used together: magnetic brakes for a smooth slowdown and friction brakes for the final stop.

A friction brake

69. An inversion is a section of a roller coaster track that turns riders upside down and then returns them

to an upright position. Different types of inversions have different names, like barrel roll or dive loop.

70. Early roller coaster loops were simple circles. To make it all the way around without stalling, coaster cars hit the circle hard and fast, shoving rider's heads into their chests as they changed direction with a sudden snap that occasionally broke bones.

The first roller coaster with a modern (clothioid) loop was Revolution at Six Flags Magic Mountain in 1976. **Vertical loops** were finally made safe and comfortable by famous roller coaster designer, Werner Stengel, when he came up with the teardrop shaped loop. He ditched the perfect circle and designed a loop with a radius of curvature that decreases as the vehicles are turned upside down. This way the g-forces at the top of the loop can be kept much closer to those of the bottom, resulting in a smooth and enjoyable experience.

71. Passengers are held safely in the roller coaster cars by primarily two methods. **Lap bar restraints** are padded bars that lower over a rider's lap, typically pressing down onto the thighs. They keep riders secured in their seats without restricting upper body movement. Lap bars are common on roller coasters with moderate speeds and forces. Riders generally find lap bars more comfortable and less restrictive, allowing for greater freedom of movement, which can enhance the sensation of airtime. However, they don't always provide as much security as shoulder restraints for more intense loops and inversions.

72. The intensity of the forces felt by the riders dictate which restraint device is used. On more intense roller coasters, **over-the-shoulder restraints** are harnesses that rest on riders' shoulders, often with padding around the neck and chest area. They lock in place across the shoulders and torso, adding stability during intense elements,

like loops and rolls. OTSRs are very secure, which is essential for high-speed loops and inversions. However, they can feel restrictive and may cause "headbanging" on rougher coasters as riders are jostled from side to side. Some newer designs use vest-style shoulder restraints, which are more flexible and prevent head contact.

Over-the-shoulder restraints on Corkscrew at Cedar Point

73. Have you ever felt like you were floating or flying on a roller coaster? That's called *airtime*! It happens when you zoom over a hill so fast that you lift off

your seat, feeling weightless for a split second. This weightless feeling happens because, at the top of a hill, the coaster is moving faster than gravity can pull you down, giving you that "butterflies in your stomach" thrill. Some coasters are famous for lots of airtime moments, making riders feel like they're popping up from their seats over and over again. But coaster designers have to keep the airtime just right. If they made it too intense, blood could rush to your head and make you feel dizzy. So, they balance the excitement for an amazing, safe ride that gives you the ultimate floating feeling.

74. Roller coasters are designed and built by a variety of different companies found all over the

world. Companies that primarily produce steel roller coasters are B&M, Intamin, Vekoma, Premier Rides, S&S, Gerstlauer, Mack Rides, and Zamperla.

75. Companies that specialize in wooden roller coasters are Philadelphia Toboggan Company (PTC), The Gravity Group (TGG) and Great Coasters International (GCI). Rocky Mountain Construction (RMC) is famous for their hybrid roller coasters.

76. **Theoretical Hourly Ride Capacity (THRC)** is the number of guests per hour that can experience an attraction under optimal operating conditions. Calculated by: Riders per bench*benches per car*cars per train*(60min/ride time minutes). Rides with low THRC tend to have the longest waits at an amusement park.

77. **ASTM F24** is a set of standards for amusement rides and devices that covers topics such as design, testing, maintenance, and safety. The ASTM F24

committee is made up of representatives from various industries, including amusement park operators, government officials, and consumer advocates. This group establishes criteria for patron restraint, acceleration limits, containment design, and clearance envelope.

78. The **clearance envelope** is a buffer of empty space around a roller coaster train that prevents riders from accidentally touching anything while it's moving.

79. Roller coaster **inspections and maintenance** are crucial for ensuring rider safety and smooth operation. Inspections happen at various intervals—daily, monthly, and annually—and are conducted by trained ride operators, engineers, and maintenance staff. Each morning, ride operators and maintenance teams do visual inspections to check for wear, loose bolts, cracks, or debris on the track. Before opening, roller coasters are test-run several times to ensure

smooth operation. Safety systems like brakes, sensors, and restraint systems are also tested.

For seasonal parks (parks not open all-year round), roller coasters undergo a detailed inspection during the off-season. The ride may be completely disassembled for an in-depth check and repair. Non-destructive testing (NDT) techniques like ultrasonic testing or magnetic particle inspection are used to detect internal flaws in metal components without damaging them. These tests help spot small cracks or weaknesses early.

80. An **E-stop** (short for **Emergency Stop**) is a safety feature on roller coasters and other rides that allows operators to quickly halt the ride in case of an emergency. When an E-stop button is pressed, it immediately shuts down the ride's movement, cutting power to key systems like the lift chain and launch mechanisms. This prevents any further motion, ensuring the safety of riders and staff. Of course, there are no brakes on the cars, so they will continue

to move until they hit the first track section that has a method to bring the car to a halt.

Roller coasters are designed to fail safe. So if there is an emergency or power is lost, the brakes will still work and will bring the cars to a stop. Power is only needed to let the cars pass through them.

81. **Theming** on a roller coaster is the use of scenery, landscaping, and a storyline to create a specific experience for riders. VelociCoaster at Universal's Islands of Adventure is themed to the Jurassic World franchise.

VelociCoaster inside the raptor pen

Record Holders and Famous Roller Coasters

82. The **oldest roller coaster**, Leap-The-Dips in Altoona, Pennsylvania, was built in 1902. Leap-The-Dips is quite tame compared to today's standards. The maximum height is an unimpressive 41 feet and the average speed a measly ten miles per hour. Leap-The-Dips did not operate in 2024 but hopefully this historic landmark will leap again soon!

83. The world's **fastest roller coaster** is Formula Rossa in Abu Dhabi, reaching speeds of 149.1 mph (240 km/h). It uses a hydraulic launch (cable) system

to obtain that blistering speed. Interestingly, the height is only 170 feet, as the designers chose to make most of the layout close to the ground rather than one big hill.

84. The **tallest roller coaster** from 2005 – 2024 was Kingda Ka at Six Flags Great Adventure, at **456 feet**. That's like if you took eleven school buses and could stack them end to end. Don't look down! *On November 14, 2024, Six Flags announced Kingda Ka is closed forever and will be removed.*

The full layout of Kingda Ka

85. The longest roller coaster in the world is Steel Dragon 2000 in Japan, stretching **8,133 feet**. That's over 27 football fields lined up end-to-end! Or, if you think about a typical school hallway, which might be around 100 feet long, this roller coaster would stretch more than 80 school hallways back-to-back!

*The tallest, fastest, and longest roller coaster records are set to be smashed by Falcon's Flight at Six Flags Qiddiya, Saudi Arabia in 2025.

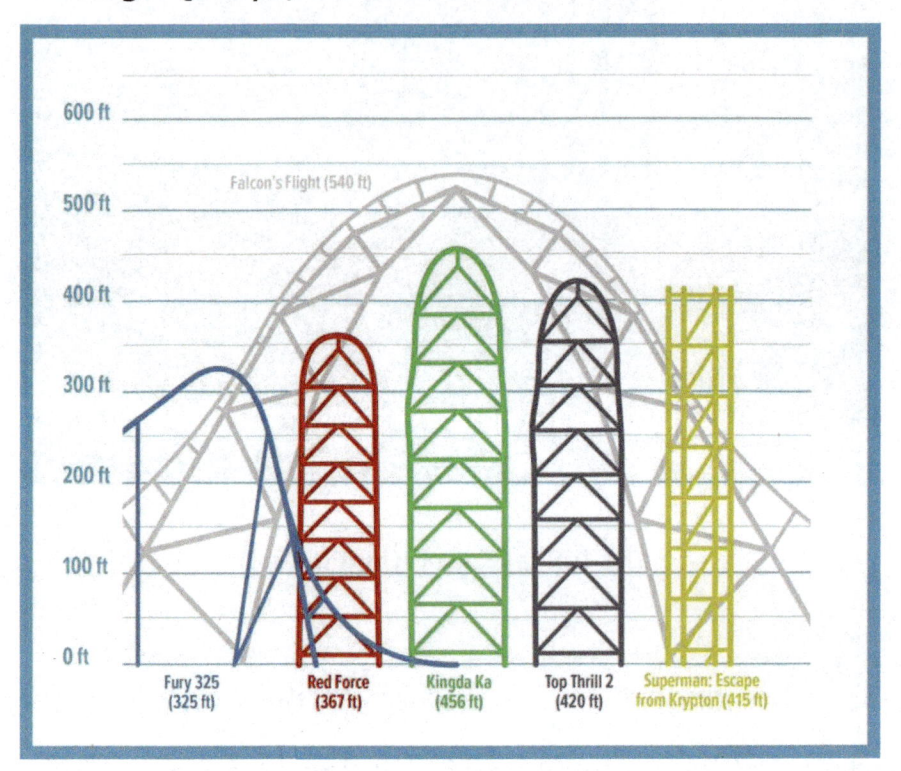

Height comparison of the tallest roller coasters

86. The Beast at Kings Island was once the world's longest wooden roller coaster and is still a fan favorite. It's especially famous for its night rides as most of the layout sprawls over a dark, hilly forest and includes multiple tunnels.

87. Today, there are three roller coasters tied for the world's **largest vertical loop** at 160 feet (48.8 meters): Flash at Lewa Adventure in China, Hyper Coaster at Lands of Legend Theme Park in Turkey, and Full Throttle at Six Flags Magic Mountain in California. Those loops are taller than the tallest point on the average roller coaster.

88. The world's **highest inversion** above the ground is the 197-foot dive drop on Kennywood's Steel Curtain, which also has the most inversions on a roller coaster in the United States. It's also the only roller coaster themed to an NFL team, the Pittsburgh Steelers. Steel Curtain was closed the entire 2024 so repairs to the structure could be made.

89. The **most inversions** on a single coaster is 14, found on *The Smiler* at Alton Towers in the United Kingdom. That's three more inversions then the next loopiest coaster in the world, and five more times upside down than the coaster with the most inversions in the United States.

Twisted track of The Smiler

90. A roller coaster referred to as "highest" might mean highest above sea level, such as Defiance at Glenwood Caverns. Situated at 7,132 feet above sea level, Defiance features a 102.3 degree, 110-foot freefall drop and boasts the steepest freefall drop in the Western United States. Built into the side of Iron Mountain, Defiance combines an incredible setting with unparalleled thrills for a one-of-a-kind ride.

91. Guardians of the Galaxy: Cosmic Rewind at EPCOT in Walt Disney World is the longest coaster in Florida and the **longest completely enclosed roller coaster** in the world at 5,577 feet. It also features controlled spinning seats.

92. The state of Pennsylvania is home to three of the ten oldest roller coasters in the world. Leap-the-Dips, Jack Rabbit at Kennywood, and Thunderhawk at Dorney Park.

93. Outlaw Run at Silver Dollar City in Branson, Missouri was the first wooden roller coaster with multiple inversions and the first looping wooden coaster since Son of Beast's loop was removed in 2006.

94. Six Flags Magic Mountain in Valencia, California has 20 roller coasters, the most of any amusement park in the world!

95. Flying Turns at Knoebels in Pennsylvania is the only **operating wooden bobsled roller** coaster today. Instead of the usual steel track, this coaster has a curved wooden track shaped like a half-pipe. The cars aren't attached to the track the same way as most coasters, so they can freely roll, just like a bobsled racing down an icy track.

96. Niagara Falls, Canada is not only home to one of the wonders of the natural world but also to another kind of wonder for roller coaster enthusiasts: The Burger King Coaster. Yes, you read that right. There is a roller coaster on top of a Burger King restaurant, and you can ride it.

97. Australia's Adventure World opened Abyss in 2013, a custom-designed Gerstlauer Euro-Fighter coaster (the first of its kind in the country). In an effort to help promote Abyss as Australia's most terrifying coaster, the park placed underwear dispensers outside the exit of the ride, stocked with packets of fresh clean white underpants. Along with the "tighty whities," the undies packets contain a fact sheet outlining all the key statistics and features relating to the ride. The park hasn't revealed how many guests have actually needed the packets.

98. The Crystal Beach Cyclone is considered to be the most extreme roller coaster ever built. The mother of all roller coasters was spawned in 1927 at Crystal Beach Amusement Park in Ontario, Canada. For over 20 years this demonic creation terrorized over five million victims, dragging them through its demented dives, twisted turns, and wickedly warped trackage.

While its 96-foot-tall lift hill may be relatively small by today's standards, the Cyclone made up for lack of height with rapid fire transitions and perverted elements, such as 80-degree banked turns, a high-speed figure-eight, jazz-track (trick track), and tiny one-foot bunny hops. Although this terrifying trip lasted only around 40 seconds after cresting the lift, there was almost no straight track to be found. The unrelenting pace made the ride so severe it was probably more than most riders could handle. In fact, what made the Cyclone even more notorious was the employment of a full-time nurse in the station to treat passengers coming off the ride. Common ailments were aches, pains, stiff necks, and fainting, either due to fear or being knocked unconscious by the ride's forces. A few accounts from actual survivors of the Cyclone claim the station constantly reeked of vomit.

99. X2 was the first 4th dimension wing coaster where the controlled spinning or rotation of the seats is in a direction that is independent of the track—hence the "fourth dimension" designation. There are two sets of rails—one supports the weight of the vehicles while the other is what makes the seats rotate. The vertical distance or displacement between the two sets of rails controls the rotation of the passengers by transforming linear motion into rotational motion, accomplished via a rack and pinion gear.

4D coaster known as X2

100. A roller coaster in Denmark might have the most ridiculous theme for a roller coaster. Hundeprutterutchebane is Danish for "Dog Fart" and is referred to as the "Dog Fart Coaster."

101. Maximum RPM, a Premier Rides coaster that operated at the now defunct Hard Rock Park in Murtle Beach, South Carolina, had probably the most unusual method for a coaster to gain its maximum

potential energy. Ladies and gentlemen, behold the Ferris wheel lift. Yes, a Ferris wheel, the popular attraction found at almost every amusement park was used to lift the convertible-styled cars to the highest point.

Roller Coaster Trivia

Test your roller coaster knowledge with these trivia questions!

1. What are the wheels located on the underside of the rails that help secure the cars to the track called?
a. Road wheels
b. Side-friction wheels
c. Upstop wheels

2. True or false: None of the top ten tallest roller coasters go upside down.

3. How many currently operating wooden roller coasters in the world go upside down?
a. 3
b. 8
c. 11

4. Which country has the most operating roller coasters?

5. What does LIM and LSM stand for?

6. What are the two primary types of brakes?

7. What does ACE stand for?

8. What does ASTM International stand for?

9. This roller coaster is located at Six Flags Great Adventure in Jackson Township, New Jersey, United States. It opened in May 2005, and reaches 128 miles per hour.

10. What does NDT stand for?

11. What is a hyper coaster?

circuit to be considered a hyper coaster.

13. True or false: A roller coaster with a steel support structure is always classified as a steel coaster.

14. How many roller coasters over 400 feet tall have ever been built?

15. How many wooden roller coasters over 200 feet tall have ever been built?

16. True or false: A floorless roller coaster allows rider's feet to dangle freely above the track.

17. Roller coasters originated in the country of _____ as ice slides.

18. True or False: The Centrifugal Railway in Frascati Garden was the first full-circuit roller coaster.

19. In 1925, the first roller coaster to break the 100-foot-tall barrier was:

a. Revere Beach Cyclone

b. Crystal Beach Cyclone

c. Coney Island Cyclone

20. Which decade was considered the first Golden Age of roller coasters?

a. 1910s

b. 1920s

c. 1930s

21. Which country opened their first wooden roller coaster in 1999?

22. **Friction** is a _____ that resists relative motion (sliding or rolling) of an object.

23. The _____ _____ is a buffer of empty space around a roller coaster train that prevents riders from accidentally touching anything while it's moving.

24. The purpose of an ARB is:

a. To catch onto the chain to lift the car up the lift hill

b. Keep the passengers inside the car

c. Prevent the car from rolling backwards down a hill

25. The most inversions on a roller coaster is:

a. 11

b. 14

c. 16

26. This side friction roller coaster opened in 1902.

27. What type of roller coaster seats riders on either side of the track?

a. wing coaster

b. double coaster

c. wishbone coaster

28. Roller coasters with the same layout are referred to as _____.

29. How many inversions does a cobra roll element have?

a. 1

b. 2

c. 3

30. Am inverted type of roller coaster is:

a. any roller coaster that goes upside down

b. where rider's feet dangle freely above the rails

c. where the vehicle hangs below the rails

31. King Kobra at Kings Dominion was the first launch coaster. The launch system was:

a. Magnets

b. Dropped weights

c. Compressed air

32. What was the first roller coaster to use a modern control system?

33. Name one of the three roller coasters currently tied for having the largest vertical loop.

34. What unit is the acceleration due to gravity measured in?

35. _____ **energy** is *stored* and based on position, while _____ **energy** is the *energy of motion.*

36. Bollinger and Mabillard (B&M) are famous for what type of roller coasters:
a. steel
b. wood
c. hybrid

37. What does THRC stand for?

38. **ASTM** _____ is a set of standards for amusement rides and devices that covers topics such as design:

a. E24

b. F25

c. D24

39. The tallest roller coaster with a chain lift is:

a. Red Force

b. Millennium Force

c. Fury 325

40. What was the first roller coaster to reach 100 miles per hour?

Mind Eraser at Six Flags Darien Lake

Roller Coaster Trivia Answers

1. c, upstop wheels
2. True
3. b, 8. Outlaw Run, Wildfire, Goliath, Hades 360, Mine Blower, Jungle Trailblaze x3
4. China, 1,670 operating roller coasters
5. Linear Induction Motor, Linear Synchronous Motor
6. Friction and magnetic
7. American Coaster Enthusiasts
8. Trick question! ASTM used to stand for American Society for Testing and Materials but now is simply known as ASTM International
9. Kingda Ka
10. Non-destructive testing
11. A roller coaster between 200 and 299 feet tall
12. False
13. False
14. Four (Top Thrill Dragster/Top Thrill 2, Kingda Ka, Superman Escape from Krypton, Falcon's Flight)
15. One, Son of Beast

17. Russia

18. False, The Aerial Walk (*Promenades Aeriennes*) was the first full-circuit roller coaster

19. a, Revere Beach Cyclone

20. b, the 1920s

21. Brazil

22. Force

23. Clearance envelope

24. c, ARB stands for anti-roll back

25. b, 14 inversions on The Smiler

26. Leap-The-Dips

27. a, wing coaster

28. Clones

29. 2 inversions

30. c

31. b

32. Matterhorn Bobsleds at Disneyland

33. Flash at Lewa Adventure in China, Hyper Coaster at Lands of Legend Theme Park in Turkey, or Full Throttle at Six Flags Magic Mountain in California

34. meters per second squared

36. a, steel

37. Theoretical Hourly Ride Capacity

38. b

39. c

40. Superman the Escape (now called Escape from Krypton)

Trivia Score

Now add up your score to see how you did!

16 – 20: Room for Improvement

You're on the right track but there's more to discover about roller coasters. Keep learning!

21 – 25: Not Bad!

You've got a fair understanding of roller coasters. Keep exploring and you'll improve even more.

26 – 30: Good Going!

You know quite a bit about roller coasters! You'll be an expert in no time.

31 – 35: Great Job!

You've got a fantastic knowledge of roller coasters. Keep up the good work!

36 – 40: You're A Roller Coaster Expert!

Wow, you really know your roller coasters. You're a true roller coaster expert.

Journal

Journal

Journal

Journal

Journal

Journal

Journal

Journal

Enjoy the Ride

Roller coaster fans are always looking for rides that are taller, faster, and even wilder than before. Every time they visit an amusement park, they want something that feels bigger and better. To keep up, theme parks are constantly trying to create "world's first" rides that are totally unique and thrilling. Even though building these rides costs a lot, parks know fans will travel far and wide to try them out. For the engineers and designers, the challenge is to make each ride more intense without sacrificing safety.

Roller coasters come in tons of different styles, and while some designs are a huge hit, others don't last because they're too expensive to keep running or just weren't a great idea. But don't worry—the evolution of roller coasters isn't slowing down anytime soon. Get ready for the awesome scream machines of the future!

Would You Like to Know More About Roller Coaster Design?

Have you ever wondered what it takes to design and build a roller coaster? At last, there's a book that shows you. A mix of engineering and art, roller coasters are complex three-dimensional puzzles consisting of thousands of individual parts. Designers spend countless hours creating and tweaking ride paths to push the envelope of exhilaration, all while maintaining the highest safety standards. ***Coasters 101: An Engineering Guide to Roller Coaster Design*** examines the numerous diverse aspects of roller coaster engineering, including some of the mathematical formulas and engineering concepts used.

A few of the many topics covered include:
- Roller coaster history
- Defining wood versus steel roller coasters
- What software roller coaster designers use
- Roller coaster physics and formulas
- Project management and construction
- Wheel design and material selection
- Track fabrication techniques
- Daily inspections and preventive maintenance
- Amusement industry safety standards
- Career advice to help you become a roller coaster engineer

And much more!

This technical guide is the most detailed roller coaster design book to date and will take you through the entire process, from concept to creation. A must read for every enthusiast and aspiring roller coaster engineer!

Get **Coasters 101: An Engineering Guide to Roller Coaster Design** from Amazon.com today.

Did You Like 101 Facts About Roller Coasters?

Before you go, I'd like to say "thank you" for purchasing my book. I know you could have picked from dozens of other books, but you took a chance on mine. So, a big thanks for ordering this book and reading all the way to the end.

Now I'd like to ask for a *small* favor. Could you please take a minute or two and leave a review for this book on Amazon.com? Your comments are really valuable because they will guide future editions of this book and I'm always striving to improve my writing.

About the Author

Nick Weisenberger creates content for Coaster101.com. He's been a member of the ASTM International F-24 committee on Amusement Rides and Devices. In August 2009, he participated in the Coasting for Kids Ride-a-thon where he endured a ten-hour marathon ride (that's 105 laps) and helped raise over $10,000 for Give Kids the World charity. When not writing or working, Nick likes to read, hike, watch football, and explore. An avid traveler, look for Nick on the midways of your local amusement park!

As of October 2024, Nick has ridden 297 different roller coasters. He knows exactly how many because he uses a spreadsheet to keep track. If you'd like to track your own coaster count, you can download a copy of his spreadsheet template here:

https://gum.co/coastercount

Books by Nick Weisenberger

25 Extreme Drop Tower Rides

50 *Ground-breaking* Roller Coasters

50 *Legendary* Roller Coasters That No Longer Exist

A Brick-by-Brick Guide to Legoland New York

Coaster Phobia: How to Get Over Your Fear of Roller Coasters

Coasters 101: An Engineer's Guide to Roller Coaster Design

Steam Trains and Monorails

The 50 Biggest Ferris Wheels Ever Built

The 50 Most *Terrifying* Roller Coasters Ever Built

The 50 Most *Unique* Roller Coasters Ever Built

Things to Do in the Smokies with Kids

My Track Record: Roller Coaster Log

101 Facts About Roller Coasters for Kids

Resources

For additional information, please check out the following tools and resources. This book wouldn't have been possible without them.

American Coaster Enthusiasts (ACE)
http://www.aceonline.org/

ASTM International
http://www.ASTM.org

International Association of Amusement Parks and Aquariums (IAAPA)
http://www.IAAPA.org/

Coaster101
http://www.Coaster101.com

Roller Coaster Database
http://www.RCDB.com

Themed Entertainment Association (TEA)
http://www.teaconnect.org/

Photography Credits

Tallest roller coaster graphic by Kyle Lindner

Wood coaster track graphic by Nick Weisenberger

Pictures by Nick Weisenberger:

Screamin' Eagle at Six Flags St. Louis

Flash: Vertical Velocity at Six Flags Great America

Corkscrew at Cedar Point

Wildifre at Silver Dollar City

Pipeline the Surf Coaster at SeaWorld Orlando

Freedom Flyer at Fun Spot America

Tidal Twist at the Columbus Zoo and Aquarium

Matterhorn Bobsleds at Disneyland

Magnum XL-200 at Cedar Point

Millennium Force at Cedar Point

Wolverine Wildcat at Michigan's Adventure

Goliath at Six Flags Over Georgia

White Lightning at Fun Spot America

Velocicoaster at Universal's Islands of Adventure

The Beast at Kings Island

Frankn' Coaster at Niagara Falls

Mind Eraser at Six Flags Darien Lake

Storm Chaser at Kentucky Kingdom

Mystery Mine at Dollywood

Flickr Pictures distributed under a Cc-BY 2.0 License:
http://creativecommons.org/licenses/by/2.0/
Knoebels, https://flic.kr/p/cB2yA7 **by Jeremy Thompson**
Hard Rock Park 067, https://flic.kr/p/5MHr8c **by** Jeremy Thompson

Wikimedia Commons Pictures
Image-Lightning Racer at Hersheypark station.jpg
Promenades Aeriennes, Jardin Baujon (roller coaster at the Folie Beaujon) Paris, c. 1820
Centrifugal Railway Detailed Sketch.jpg
Switchback Railroad, Mauch Chunk, Pa., U.S.A, from Robert N. Dennis collection of stereoscopic views.png
Thompsons Switchback Railway 1884.jpg
Anti Roll-Back.png **by MrEpFan**
Leap The Dips (Lakemont Park).jpg **By Bhakta Dano.**
Formula Rossa coaster.jpg
Formula Rossa launched roller coaster
Kingda Ka (Full Layout).JPG
Kingda Ka's **full circuit by** Coasterman1234
Kennywood - 48555719127.jpg
The Steel Curtain by Roller Coaster Philosophy
Batwingcobra.jpg
Image of the batwing/cobra roll on The Smiler as it was on the 16th March 2013 by AAdamsRC
X2 at Six Flags Magic Mountain (13208066443).jpg
Six Flags Magic Mountain by Jeremy Thompson

Printed in Dunstable, United Kingdom